WORLD SET FREE

Bryn Magnus

BROADWAY PLAY PUBLISHING INC
224 E 62nd St, NY, NY 10065
www.broadwayplaypub.com
info@broadwayplaypub.com

WORLD SET FREE
© Copyright 2003 by Bryn Magnus

Cover art by Dave Buchen

First printing: November 2016
I S B N: 978-0-88145-683-7

Book design: Marie Donovan
Word processing: Microsoft Word
Typographic controls: Adobe InDesign
Typeface: Palatino
Printed and bound in the U S A

WORLD SET FREE was first produced at the
Steppenwolf Theater in Chicago. The play opened 25
February 2003 and closed 15 March 2003. The cast and
creatives contributors were:

LEO SZILARD .... Patrick Dollymore
DOMINIQUE ....Linara Washington
JANOS.. Hans Fleischman
VIOLETTA..Katie Johnston
VITO .... Eli Goodman
ENRICO FERMI .... James Elly
LAURA FERMI .... Charin Alvarez
ARTHUR COMPTON...................................... Wayne Brown

Director .... Hallie Gordon
Scenic design...Stephanie Nelson
Costume design ....Lynn Koscielniak
Lighting design .... Allison Heryer
Sound design...Josh Schmidt
Stage manager..Michelle Medvin
Dramaturg ....Rosie Forrest
Choreographer...Ann Boyd

CHARACTERS & SETTING

LEO SZILARD, *Jewish Hungarian-born physicist and inventor who conceived the nuclear chain reaction that resulted in the atomic bomb*

DOMINIQUE, *high school student from Back of the Yards south side Chicago*

JANOS, *high school student from Back of the Yards south side Chicago*

VIOLETTA, *high school student from Back of the Yards south side Chicago*

VITO, *high school student from Back of the Yards south side Chicago*

ENRICO FERMI, *Italian physicist who created the world's first nuclear reactor that became the basis for the atomic bomb*

LAURA FERMI, ENRICO FERMI's *wife and confidante*

ARTHUR COMPTON *Leader of the Manhattan Project's Metallurgical Lab and host to* LEO SZILARD *and* ENRICO FERMI *at the University of Chicago*

Place: the University of Chicago and in the neighborhood called "back of the yards".

PROLOGUE: FIRESIDE CHAT

(The stage is dark. A pulsing, driving swing beat grows in the distance around a collage of sounds of war and industry. The following might be heard altogether, or cut up.)

FRANKLIN DELANO ROOSEVELT: My fellow Americans: Powerful and resourceful gangsters have banded together to make war upon the whole human race. Their challenge has now been flung at the United States of America. The fleet at Pearl Harbor has been treacherously attacked. Many American soldiers and sailors have been killed by enemy action. American ships have been sunk; American airplanes have been destroyed.

The Congress and the people of the United States have accepted that challenge.

Together with other free peoples, we are now fighting to maintain our right to live among our world neighbors in freedom, in common decency, without fear of assault.

The course our enemies have followed in the past ten years is a collaboration so well calculated that all the continents of the world, and all the oceans, are now considered by the Axis strategists as one gigantic battlefield.

It is all of one pattern.

We are now in this war. We are all in it—all the way. Every single man, woman and child is a partner in the most tremendous undertaking of our American history. We must share together the bad news and the

good news, the defeats and the victories—the changing
fortunes of war.

SCENE: A DANGEROUS IDEA IN AMERICA

*(At rise, swing beat drives through an eerie light. Upstage
right, figures dance. Lights brighten.)*

*(The dance is swing with snatches of contemporary juke
moves. It reaches a lively pitch and then suspends.)*

*(LEO enters with a suitcase. Kids grab his suitcase and razz
him.)*

LEO: You never know what someone else might
invent. Someone invented the electric guitar, someone
else invented aspirin. Completely different people
invented the movies and nylon stockings and fountain
pens and baby food and caesar salad and coca cola
and eyeglasses and glass eyes. You wonder how it is
possible to invent paper or the telephone.
And someone invented walking. And now you're just
out walking. Walking and thinking. Thinking about
atoms or chocolate or two dinners instead of one or
the horror of exposed gristle in the devastated arm of
a screaming soldier. You're just walking and thinking
about war and the architecture of snowflakes, and
suddenly a bolt of lightening shoots through you—
energy—energy like a diamond leaping apart into a
twinkling dust of light that rips your body, splits your
blood in two burning waves that part leaving an idea
like Moses standing in an empty sea.
An idea so primal that it stands alone. You can walk
around it, and look at it from all sides. People around
you start to notice a strange light coming from your
eyes. You want to describe it but you can't. You want
to tell them so badly about the incredible, sparkling,
bewildering idea in your brain. There is no language.

(LEO *has gotten his suitcase back, and has crossed the stage to his office. He is now on the phone.*)

LEO: You first have to invent the language. But as you're inventing the language, you stop yourself because what if just by telling someone about this idea, it gets in their brain too. The pump? The refrigerator pump? NO I AM NOT TALKING ABOUT THE EINSTEIN-SZILARD REFRIGERATOR PUMP! Alright. I'm sorry I yelled. Me too. Alright. I'm just sensitive about the pump because everyone teases me about the pump. The pump, the pump. I love you too. Don't tell anyone we talked.

(*Cross fade. Music rises up and then resolves into a muted, driving beat.*)

YOUTH CULTURE CHICAGO

(JANOS *and* VITO *and* DOMINIQUE *and* VIOLETTA *move downstage.* JANOS *and* VITO *pretend not to see the girls.*)

VITO: You know what I hate, Janos?

JANOS: Tell me, Vito.

VITO: I hate waiting for our Chicks.

DOMINIQUE: Vi, they hate waiting for us. Doesn't that just touch ya?

VIOLETTA: I'm working up a tear, Nique.

VITO: We're out here waitin and wonderin where's our chicks? Where's our Chicks? School's gotta be out by now, right? Time's tickin and where's our chickens? OHHHH. Here they are now.

DOMINIQUE: Yeah, here we are. You near sighted?

JANOS: How was school, Violetta?

VIOLETTA: Dull without you, Janos.

JANOS: Nah.

VIOLETTA: Yeah.

VITO: What about you, duchess, you miss me all day?

DOMINIQUE: Yeah, Vito, I got so distracted by your absence I could barely get an A in calculus.

JANOS: I miss going to school.

VITO: What? We only been out a week.

JANOS: A whole long week.

VITO: You got the smarts real bad.

JANOS: So I like to read.

VITO: So I don't.

VIOLETTA: I like to read too. Don't you, Nique?

DOMINIQUE: No.

VIOLETTA: NIQUE!

VITO: The things I want to know, I can just feel.

DOMINIQUE: Hands off Romeo. I'm saving myself.

VITO: What for?

DOMINIQUE: Posterity.

JANOS: I feel things when I read.

VIOLETTA: Yeah me too. I feel words.

JANOS: Yeah?

VITO: I feel the wall I lean against corner of 50th and Bosworth.

DOMINIQUE: A wall that was in grave danger of the crumble before you came along?

VITO: That's the story mornin glory.

VIOLETTA: What about you, Janos? What do you do all day now that you don't go to school?

JANOS: You know. Read.

VIOLETTA: All day?

JANOS: I stare at the wall too.

DOMINIQUE: Vito's wall?

JANOS: No. The wall of my bedroom.

VIOLETTA: You just stare at the wall?

JANOS: I stare at it and think.

VIOLETTA: What about?

VITO: You.

JANOS: No, man. Yeah, but. I think about what I read. And the war.

VITO: You know what I'm thinking? I'm thinking of doing something. What are you girls doing right now.

VIOLETTA: My mom's signed me up at the Red Cross to roll bandages.

VITO: You too, Nique?

DOMINIQUE: I go where Vi goes. You guys should come.

VITO: I'm not gonna roll bandages. Come on. Let's go do somethin. Can't we do somethin?

DOMINIQUE: Ever hear of the war effort, Vito?

VITO: Course.

DOMINIQUE: Whad'you hear?

VITO: Be nice, Nique, me and Janos are G Is now. That's why we dropped school.

DOMINIQUE: No joke? When do you go?

VITO: Thing is we got to advance the spark here at home for a few months…

JANOS: I told 'em we were seventeen. I didn't know I was supposed to lie when we got to recruitment.

VITO: So now we got to wait till our birthdays.

DOMINIQUE: Heroic. So why not come roll bandages with us?

VITO: Cause I'm no cream puff.

VIOLETTA: What about you, Janos?

JANOS: I just don't think it's a good idea to roll bandages if you're going to be fighting—like a jinx or something. I don't know.

VIOLETTA: I can dig that. Man! It's going to be strange when you guys hop the drink. Me and Nique back here watching the newsreels about you guys over there. I guess then it'll be our turn to wait.

JANOS: Do you hate waiting?

VIOLETTA: It won't be so bad, I bet. Every winter I wait for spring and it's not so bad. But I hear it's cold over there.

JANOS: Aww, don't bring me down with that cold.

VIOLETTA: You don't like the cold? I'll keep you warm.

JANOS: How you gonna keep me warm when I'm over there?

VIOLETTA: I'll knit you a blanket.

VITO: She's gonna knit him a little blankey.

VIOLETTA: Probably I won't, but I'll feel bad about it.

VITO: Come on! We got to do somethin fun right now. Stop thinking about war and being cold and us over there and you over here. Let's jump or somethin!

DOMINIQUE: Jumpin will keep you warm, huh Vito.

VITO: I'm hot blooded, Nique, think you ought to know.

DOMINIQUE: I know. I can feel it from here, but we're signed up with the Red Cross and we gotta do our part.

VITO: What about later?

DOMINIQUE: What do you have in mind?

VITO: You know what I have in mind, but what say we just take in a show or somethin.

JANOS: I want to see a show.

VITO: Mash me a fiver and I'll spring for the four of us.

JANOS: I can't, I got the shorts.

VITO: Me too.

DOMINIQUE: Me too.

VIOLETTA: So do I. Hey, why aren't you guys working? You guys should be working now that you don't go to school.

DOMINIQUE: Yeah, Vito.

VITO: Yeah, well, you go roll your bandages, duchess, and I'll be sure and get to work on gettin to work.

DOMINIQUE: Yeah, right.

VIOLETTA: Meet you later, Janos?

JANOS: Right here.

VIOLETTA: Right here.

(DOMINIQUE *and* VIOLETTA *exit.*)

(*Cross fade. Beat rises intertwined with city sounds and growing aria.*)

SCENE: GETTING TO WORK IN CHICAGO

(ENRICO *and* LAURA FERMI *enter with a suitcase. They've just stepped off the train. They see* JANOS *and* VITO. ENRICO *is about to talk to them when* DOMINIQUE *and* VIOLETTA *enter.* ENRICO *and* LAURA *watch the youth flirt.*)

(LEO *enters downstage right and meets* ENRICO *and* LAURA *center.*)

LEO: Fermi.

ENRICO: Szilard. You remember my wife, Laura.

LEO: Of course. Have you been liking America?

ENRICO: *(Simultaneous with* LAURA*)* Yes!

LAURA: *(Simultaneous with* ENRICO*)* No!

ENRICO: Laura?

LAURA: Enrico? I'm worried about our Italy and our families. All we hear are bad things about Fascist midgets attacking Europe. Our children are terrified.

ENRICO: In Chicago they will grow to feel safe.

LAURA: Do you know?

ENRICO: New York was hard on you, I know. A giant speaking a new language.

LAURA: It wasn't New York, Enrico, it was the other wives of the scientists. You were working and talking about new elements and new physics, and the they were talking to me about Gary? Gary Grant?

LEO: Cary Grant.

LAURA: Cary Grant and cupcakes.

ENRICO: They were welcoming you, Laura.

LAURA: Welcome with cupcakes?

ENRICO: Chicago will be better, I promise.

(A radio plays swing loud and VITO *comes into the orbit of the adults.)*

VITO: Man, do you dig the crazy jump? Benny Goodman was a very good ear! Do you?

DOMINIQUE: Vito! *(To the adults)* We're sorry, he's a bit of a stud.

VITO: Maybe they want to jump, Dominique— *(To* LAURA*)* you want to jump?

LAURA: I don't understand.

VITO: Dance, hoof it, fly the kicks.

LAURA: No thank you.

ENRICO: Young man—

VITO: Oh, you wanna jump? Come on—I'll teach ya.

ENRICO: No. Yes, but we're waiting. I'm Enrico Fermi—

VITO: Would I know it if I knew ya?

DOMINIQUE: Vito! Make tracks. Leave Mrs and Mister alone. Next time I'll bring the leash. Sorry again.

*(*DOMINIQUE *leads* VITO *back to the pack.)*

ENRICO: America—would I know it if I knew it? Laura, you see. It's so young and enthusiastic, freedom of speech, freedom of expression, the music, the ideas, the energy.

LAURA: Go on Enrico, hoof. Hoof.

ENRICO: We are going to have such an amazing life here, Laura. Come on let's jump!

LAURA: No jumping, no thank you.

LEO: Fermi, by the way, I meant to congratulate you on the Nobel, Enrico. Stockholm, Sweden. The Nobel. I read about it.

ENRICO: Thank you. Yes. It was…it was…

LEO: The Nobel. You must be proud of your husband, Laura.

LAURA: Of course. And I usually love him.

ENRICO: Usually?

LAURA: *(To* LEO*)* Not when Enrico wants us to be a good American family with hamburgers and ketchup. I am Italian, and sometimes hamburgers and ketchup infuriates me, so I take my revenge.

LEO: By not loving him?

LAURA: No, with Pollo alla Cacciatora con Aglio!

*(*ENRICO *puts his arm around* LAURA.*)*

LEO: Aglio?

ENRICO: Garlic.

LEO: Delicious sounding revenge.

ENRICO: How is the thinking, Leo?

LEO: Abundant.

ENRICO: Of course, but are you thinking up anything good?

LEO: I can't tell you.

ENRICO: Another one of your secrets?

LEO: Of course.

ENRICO: You can't patent secrets.

LEO: I patent my ideas to protect them and make money. Secrets are for defeating the Fascists. We can't tell them how we intend to do it.

ENRICO: Leo, do you truthfully think that what we are proposing to do here is possible?

LEO: You don't believe it is? Hitler does.

LAURA: What does Hitler believe?

ENRICO: Hitler really believes in this?

LEO: Now is not the time to talk about this.

LAURA: Enrico.

ENRICO: Laura, please. Hitler really believes?

LEO: Don't you read the publications? Heisenberg, Otto Hahn and Fritz Strassmann are in Germany already working on it.

ENRICO: Strassmann—

LAURA: Are you excluding me from this conversation?

LEO: We're trying to.

ENRICO: I'm not!

LEO: You should be, Enrico. If you don't understand the gravity of the situation—who will?

ENRICO: So we are in a race against Hitler?

LEO: Yes.

LAURA: Race to what?

ENRICO: Laura, shh. What does that mean for publishing our work?

LEO: The value of some things are better kept from the world.

ENRICO: If we don't publish, who will know how the ideas advanced?

LEO: We are not doing this to be stroked like infants.

ENRICO: INFANT?! *Mi scusi? Siete un infante* rude—

LAURA: Enrico. Stop.

ENRICO: Infant, Laura?

LAURA: You see how well you are already working together.

LEO: We are?

LAURA: Yes. A little fire between friends keeps them warm.

LEO: I think better in warm bathwater.

ENRICO: I think better when I work.

LAURA: Enrico told me that you were an ingenious inventer, Leo.

LEO: Fermi, I hope you have not been Goddamn talking about this work with your wife!

LAURA: He told me you are going to um…*dia la nuova vita a*, to the Einstein-Szilard refrigerator pump project.

LEO: Oh. Oh how funny. Enrico told you to say that, right?

LAURA: You think I need my husband to help me tell a joke?

LEO: Well, laugh, laugh, one day the Einstein-Szilard pump will be cooling refrigerators around the world and that is no secret.

ENRICO: I don't think scientists, especially physicists should patent their work.

LEO: Really? How else are you supposed to buy yourself time to think?

ENRICO: Win the Nobel.

(VITO, JANOS, DOMINIQUE *and* VIOLETTA *have begun dancing again and* ENRICO *is enthralled. He works hard on mimicing the dancers.*)

VITO: Do you DIG IT?!

ENRICO: I do dig it!

LAURA: He digs, and my heart falls in all the holes.

(*The teenagers sweep* ENRICO *into their fold. He dances.*)

LAURA: Enrico! Enrico!

LEO: Let him go, Laura. You know, even in America there is no such thing as free speech. Everything you

say has consequences. There is, of course, an enormous
difference between the squirrel fever talk of a jive-
hound coke'n'soda teen-ager speaking slang to friends
about a fully-packed fly chick or swooney Romeo, and
the open discussion of potentially dangerous ideas in a
publication that German scientists can read.

LAURA: I know that you and Enrico are here to do big
work, but I wish—

LEO: The consequences of free speech can be
wonderful—you might get kissed perfectly, but I fear
something much worse.

LAURA: You don't need to lecture me, Leo.

LEO: Thank you. I know that Enrico brings his notes to
you and the two of you work together and talk.

LAURA: You don't want me to talk to Enrico?

LEO: You must be strong. Even if he begins a discourse
in all innocence.

LAURA: Stop him?

LEO: Yes.

LAURA: So that you can work in secret?

LEO: Yes.

LAURA: The Fascists thrive on secrets, Leo.

LEO: We are not fascists.

LAURA: Yes? What are you?

LEO: Physicists. (*He picks up his suitcase, looks around.*)

(ENRICO *swings around and catches* LAURA.)

ENRICO: Laura! Like this.

LAURA: Oh, Rico, no…no, *non lo fa prego.* L'OH alright,
signore dancer.

(ENRICO *takes* LAURA *in his arms to teach her the moves.*)

VITO: Like this Professor, like this!

(VITO *demonstrates and* ENRICO *mimics.* LAURA *tries.*)

DOMINIQUE: Here. Watch. It's like this.

(DOMINIQUE *grabs* ENRICO *and leads him through some moves.* LAURA *watches.*)

JANOS: Did you ever?

VIOLETTA: No I never!

VITO: That's the stuff, you're hot, Professor, HOT.

ENRICO: The energy. The energy—Laura.

(ENRICO *grabs* LAURA *and they try again.*)

VIOLETTA: There's no douse on your glim, Professor. Mrs. That's the ticket.

ENRICO: Energy equals mass times the speed of light squared!

JANOS: You shred it, wheat.

LAURA: Vigorous, Enrico, no?

ENRICO: Chicago Laura!

LAURA: Yes, Enrico.

ENRICO: It is good. America is the energy of youth.

(*Music transitions into something slower.* ENRICO *and* LAURA *dance slow.* LEO *watches.* VITO, JANOS, VIOLETTA, DOMINIQUE *work moves upstage right.*)

(ARTHUR COMPTON *enters at a gallop.*)

ARTHUR: Here I am. Here I am. Oh my. I'm sorry to keep you waiting. Doctor Szilard, Doctor Arthur Holly Compton. Welcome to Chicago.

(ARTHUR *and* LEO *shake hands.*)

ARTHUR: Doctor Fermi, Doctor Arthur Holly Compton. Welcome to Chicago.

(ARTHUR *and* ENRICO *shake hands.*)

ARTHUR: Mrs Fermi, Doctor Arthur Holly Compton. Welcome to Chicago. *(He takes her hand.)* Welcome to Chicago and to the University of Chicago. Beautiful. Beautiful. Stockyards and all. At any rate. I trust you enjoyed your train ride. Mrs Fermi? Yes? No?

LAURA: I enjoy scenery, just not so much of it, and I was cold.

ARTHUR: Yes. Well then. Certainly. I need to discuss business with your husband and Doctor Szilard.

LAURA: The secret business? Ah—ha ha ha.

LEO: Would you mind standing twenty feet in that direction, Laura?

ENRICO: *Voi serie rude di drool sulla faccia di vecchia capra.*

LAURA: Enrico?!

LEO: What did he say?

LAURA: That you were a rude string of drool on the face of an old goat.

ENRICO: Laura!

LAURA: I'm sure you didn't mean any offense, Enrico.

ARTHUR: I'm sure none of us has meant any offense. It's just that we have some dull science to talk about, Mrs Fermi.

LAURA: I don't find science dull at all.

ENRICO: I dictate my notes to Laura every day.

LAURA: I am fascinated by ideas, Doctor Compton.

ARTHUR: Oh. That's to your credit. However your husband won't be able to discuss his notes with you for some time. We're working on a marvelous surprise and we don't want to spoil it.

LAURA: Are you patronizing me, Doctor Compton?

ARTHUR: No! Not at all. Come now.

LAURA: Doctor Compton?

ARTHUR: Yes. I'm sorry. I've been caught. I don't mean to patronize you. I'm not well practiced in the art of asking a wife to relinquish her husband. It's just that our work is urgent, and we have matters to discuss that are…urgent, and—

LAURA: Yes?

(ARTHUR *appeals to* ENRICO.)

ENRICO: Laura. For a moment. Please. Wait over there. *(Tenderly) Con tenerezza?*

LAURA: This is tenderness? Enrico, no, this is hamburgers and ketchup.

(LAURA *paces out twenty steps. When* ARTHUR *is sure she can't hear, he begins.)*

ARTHUR: As you know, I've been appointed official investigative chairman, committee head executor and top man of the National Academy of Particle Scientists Diligently Laboring in Secret to Evaluate, Measure, Assess, Address, Consider and Arrange for the use of Particles for Energy and Weaponry to Vanquish Agents, Maniacs, and Foreign Hostiles Impeding the way of Life and Liberty of Loyal Citizens of the United States of America. Code named the Metallugical Laboratory. Or, Met Lab.
Doctor Szilard. You are designated the Chief Advocate of the Imagination, the Letter Writer Nonpareil, the Commander of Important Phone Calls and Indispensable Master Suggestion Maker and Memo Proliferator. You will also be the project Nag. Not my words. These come down from above. You will be known as Leo, or Doctor Szilard, or Szilard or the Hungarian. Doctor Fermi, your designation is as follows: The Highly Respected Emancipator of the Particle, the Awe Inspiring Poet of All Measurements,

the Tireless and Dutiful Marshall of Lab Procedure and Execution, and the Scientist To Whom We All Defer. You will be known as Enrico, or Doctor Fermi, or the Italian Navigator.

(LEO *raises his hand.*)

ARTHUR: Hoo, question already?

LEO: *(Angrily)* Who came up with these lousy designations?

ARTHUR: Doctor Szilard. Leo. You have not been designated as the questioner of designations. *(An attempt at a joke for him)* As top man that would be me.

LEO: And who are you?

ARTHUR: *(Testily)* Arthur Holly Compton, as you know.

LEO: And what have you done?

ARTHUR: The list is long, but at the very top sits the Nobel Prize.

LEO: Wasn't that fifteen years ago?

ARTHUR: Is it that long already? Ah gentlemen, the Nobel.

ENRICO: Yes, the Nobel.

ARTHUR: What an amazing award and treasured distinction.

ENRICO: Laura and I owe our lives to it.

ARTHUR: It's just a phenomenal prize.

LEO: Yes, it seems that winning it does not stop with winning it.

ARTHUR: Yes. Sorry. Now.

LEO: It galls me to have been left out of the designation process, Compton.

ARTHUR: The United States Department of War now owns this project. And I remind that it does so in large part because of your efforts. Your letters. Your phone calls. Your memos. Your prodigious habit of nagging. Hence…

LEO: I didn't nag the government to take over. Just to get involved.

(ARTHUR *pulls a paper from his pocket.*)

ARTHUR: The government's involvement is taking over. Listen, the F B I gave me this: *(Reads)* "Mister Szilard is believed to be named Szilard."

LEO: GIVE ME THAT! *(Grabs paper, reads)* "Employment of this person on secret work is not recommended." WHAT!

ARTHUR: Here is what they had to say about you, Doctor Fermi: *(Reads)* "Fermi has been a Nobel Prize winner. His associates like him personally and greatly admire his intellectual ability. But employment of this person on secret work is not recommended."

LEO: This is ridiculous! Einstein and I wrote the letter to the President that started this project.

ARTHUR: Ridiculous or not, the F B I's new top man, Leiutenant Colonel J Edgar Hoover, is giving us a short leash. So. Now. I would like to talk about secrecy. Fine. Let me just be clear. Talk to no one outside of Met Lab. Submit no work for publication.
Understood?

ENRICO: It helps me to talk to Laura. Her perspective is refreshing—

LEO: NO! That means NO, Fermi. No discussions before dinner, over dinner, or after dinner, no casual conversation, even if you trust her. I don't want the F B I to pull me off the project because your wife mentioned something to the postman.

ENRICO: Laura can understand the gravity of the work.

LEO: Goddamn it. Arthur?

ARTHUR: Again, Leo. I wish you would let me practice my designated task, and you can practice yours.

LEO: I am. I'm nagging.

ARTHUR: Right. Well.

LEO: I invented secrecy. The F B I, puh!

ARTHUR: We're top secret henceforth. The very top of secrecy. It is a rare place. We are lucky to be here. Doctor Fermi? You see?

(ENRICO *looks at* LAURA.)

ENRICO: I don't like it, I don't like it. We came here together.

ARTHUR: Listen. I've roughed out a time frame. Determine whether a chain reaction is possible by July '42; achieve the first chain reaction by January '43; extract the first plutonium from uranium by January, '44; and by December'45—

LEO: Incredibly that is the exact timeframe that I outlined in a memo to the President.

ARTHUR: Good, then you're behind it. Now. Doctor Fermi?

ENRICO: This is it then. After this we are committed?

LEO: Yes. Come on Fermi.

ENRICO: Oh, this is easy for you, you don't have a wife, you love secrets.

LEO: But I hate Fascism.

ENRICO: So do I.

LEO: Well then? Enrico, we need you.

ENRICO: Alright. I begin in earnest right now.

ARTHUR: Good. Good.

(LAURA *wanders over and* ARTHUR *gets nervous.*)

ARTHUR: Ah, Mrs Fermi. As I was saying. I think you'll find this a good city. Good people. The University is full of good young scientists.

LAURA: Like those scientists over there? *(She indicates* VITO, JANOS, DOMINIQUE *and* VIOLETTA.)

ARTHUR: Ah, ha-ha… No. Those are not scientists.

VITO: Yeah we are, I'm a doctor of the piccolo tumble.

JANOS: Yeah, we're all PhDs in being Hep Gees.

LEO: Have you been listening to our conversation?!

VIOLETTA: Don't let these boys Jeff you, Mister, they're just yard dogs sniffing for some zeal.

ARTHUR: *(To the youth)* Take your sniffs elsewhere. Now. Scatter.

(They don't move)

ARTHUR: Well. And. Come summer, the 55th street beach is only a short stroll. I know Doctor Fermi that you like to swim. So. You should get settled and we'll begin in the morning. Again, welcome. And Mrs. Fermi, we might not see a lot of each other in the next few months, but I will endeavor to make the experience a pleasant one when we do. Goodnight.

VITO: Goodnight, Professor. *(To* JANOS *and* VIOLETTA, *and* DOMINIQUE*)* Goodnight, Professor. Professors.

JANOS: Professor, in the present spirit of mutual confidence and mutual encouragement we go forward.

VIOLETTA: After you Mister Roosevelt.

JANOS: You first.

VIOLETTA: Goodnight to you too, Professor.

VITO: And to you too.

DOMINIQUE: Leash it.

(The adults ignore this. ARTHUR *begins to exit.)*

LEO: I want to talk with you Arthur.

ARTHUR: Arthur. Is fine. Fine.

*(*ARTHUR *and* LEO *exit together.)*

(Cross fade)

SCENE: ENRICO AND LAURA FERMI

(Stage left, ENRICO *and* LAURA *become visible in low light. An Italian aria drifts low. There is a sense of passing time.)*

LAURA: It's cold Enrico. *(Perhaps in Italian)*

ENRICO: Is it?

LAURA: I'm cold. *(In Italian)*

*(*ENRICO *holds out his hand to feel the air.)*

ENRICO: But it's really only forty-six degrees, which for February in Chicago—a long way from the equator—is quite mild.

LAURA: Forty-six degrees?

ENRICO: Ah, I mean forty-six degrees Fahrenheit.

LAURA: Fahrenheit, Enrico? You truly have become an American.

ENRICO: So have you.

LAURA: To a smaller degree Celsius.

ENRICO: Hm?

LAURA: To a small degree Celsius.

ENRICO: Celsius would be seven-point-eight degrees. *(He turns and looks at her.)*

LAURA: It was a joke. An American joke, a joke in Chicago, you could laugh.

ENRICO: Celsius is a joke?

LAURA: It was a joke. You know, a small one.

ENRICO: Not terribly funny by my estimation.

LAURA: Estimation? Not from you, Enrico. Please, an exact measurement of just how humorless my joke was. Was it not terribly funny to the power of 5? 6?

ENRICO: Ah, a second joke.

LAURA: Yes, a cold one—

ENRICO: You should go inside if you're cold!

(ENRICO *motions for* LAURA *to go in. She doesn't.*)

LAURA: Enrico, the mountains by Lake Como? We were hiking—God, three years ago already—spring of '39. You, marching upward— racing—and I begged you to stop so I could get my legs back. And you said, "We stop only when we get back to the bottom." And you looked at me—the professor full of disdain—your sweater buttoned up all the way, but then you sneaked that other look, that wet starry look that we both knew. My heart was burning in my cheeks, and the grass was soft…I love Italy and Lake Como.

(*Music fades.*)

ENRICO: There are plenty of mountains and lakes in America.

LAURA: In Chicago?

ENRICO: Lake Michigan.

LAURA: Can you hear the wind on the lake?

ENRICO: Yes.

LAURA: We'll talk about the wind, and our children— there is much we can talk about.

ENRICO: Yes, Laura, we will make it work.

LAURA: For how long?

ENRICO: Until the research is complete.

LAURA: What could you be researching? Let me think…there's uranium, and….

ENRICO: Please don't.

LAURA: It must be a weapon. If you're all so afraid that Hitler might get his hands on it.

(ENRICO *looks around.*)

ENRICO: We can not have this conversation, Laura. It is actually illegal for me to talk to you about it.

LAURA: Illegal? For a husband to talk to his wife.

ENRICO: About this.

LAURA: Why? Who would I tell? The bus driver? Or is the Government afraid I will scream out the secret when I am in the throes of passion? Yes! YES! IT'S E=MC2!

ENRICO: Don't be ridiculous. This is the opposite of ridiculous.

LAURA: The opposite of ridiculous is…?

ENRICO: Very grave.

LAURA: No, Enrico, the opposite of ridiculous is intimate. Intimacy.

ENRICO: Remind me.

LAURA: This is intimacy. (*She kisses* ENRICO)

ENRICO: I am doing work for which there is no measure.

LAURA: Work that Enrico Fermi can not measure!?

ENRICO: (*Serious*) Laura—you're shivering

LAURA: You are grave and I am cold. Come, please, it is time to eat— it would be nice if you joined your family for dinner. We can discuss the nice snow. Only twenty steps in this direction.

(LAURA *exits.* VITO *appears behind* ENRICO *and lets him pass.*)

VITO: Troubles at home, mister?

ENRICO: What?

VITO: Hard times with the old lady? I heard.

ENRICO: You heard? Who are you?

VITO: I've seen worse. I live back of the yards. Your domestics look schmaltzando compared to my old man and old lady.

ENRICO: They fight?

VITO: Does Dempsey fight?

ENRICO: Yes.

VITO: Okay then.

ENRICO: Maybe there are things your father can't tell your mother and she doesn't like that.

VITO: Maybe he can't tell her if it was two or three gallons of wine he drank—that kind of thing?

ENRICO: No, not that kind of thing.

VITO: That is a Chianti kind of thing.

ENRICO: Chianti right now sounds good.

VITO: Want to come over?

ENRICO: No. Thank you.

VITO: Reet, my old man wouldn't pass the bottle anyway.

ENRICO: Why does he drink all that wine?

VITO: That would be working in the yards.

ENRICO: The yards?

VITO: Stock yards. Slaughter.

ENRICO: That's not really something he can talk about with your mother.

VITO: You kiddin me? Pa stopped talking a long time ago. Now he yells. Cook the Goddamn meat! I bring home the Goddamn meat! You cook the Goddamn meat!

ENRICO: Everyone needs to find a way to talk.

VITO: Hey, you want to slide your jive to me—I'm all ears.

ENRICO: Do you know anything about physics?

VITO: Physics—shmysics, I know how to dance and Bennie Goodman is who taught me.

(VITO *does a few steps.* ENRICO *mimics.*)

VITO: Not bad, brighty.

ENRICO: Brighty?

VITO: Yeah, smart guy, bright, a brighty.

ENRICO: American slang. Do you go the University?

VITO: University? I just dropped out of high school to go into the army.

ENRICO: You're young.

VITO: Not too young to fight…in a few months.

LAURA: *(From offstage)* Enrico. Please come. Please. *Con tenerezza?*

VITO: You must be a newlywed.

ENRICO: Why do you say that?

VITO: The old lady askin please.

ENRICO: We've been married seven years.

VITO: Then she's a nice old lady and you should make tracks.

ENRICO: Enrico Fermi. *(He holds out his hand.)*

VITO: Vito Ditaglia.

(ENRICO *and* VITO *shake.* VITO *stage right.* ENRICO *begins working stage left.*)

(*Lights fade out. Swing beat rises.* ENRICO *is working.*)

SCENE: BACK OF THE YARDS

(*Lights rise on the Back of the Yards.* JANOS, VIOLETTA, *and* DOMINIQUE *hang out at* JANOS' *house. Sounds of the city mix with swing*)

VIOLETTA: Janos?

JANOS: Yeah?

VIOLETTA: What you readin?

JANOS: H G Wells, *World Set Free.*

VIOLETTA: Any good?

JANOS: It's H G Wells, isn't it?

(VITO *enters.*)

VITO: Alreet, boys and girls now pay attention.
This one comes straight from the Harlem Congeroo Dancers.

VIOLETTA: Aw did you? Did you catch Swing Lear at the Chicago Theater?

VITO: Vi, you know I did.

VIOLETTA: Oh man!

JANOS: Tell us another one while that one's still warm, Vito.

DOMINIQUE: Swing Lear?

VIOLETTA: These killer-diller dancers from New York called the Harlem Congeroos are in Chicago doing swing Shakespeare. What's that got to do with the War! That's my mom's line when I ask her if I can go.

DOMINIQUE: I want to see that!

VITO: Where do you think I got these East Coast moves? *(He shows some moves.)*

JANOS: Jive righteous, but Chicago has moves of its own. Footwork. *(He shows his moves.)*

DOMINIQUE: Where'd you get the cabbage to see the Harlem Congeroos anyway?

VITO: I got a job.

DOMINIQUE: Oh Lord and Butler, I didn't know leanin on your wall at Bosworth and 50th paid anything.

VITO: I work at the University.

JANOS: *(Mocking)* I work at the university.

VITO: I do work at the University.

JANOS: Do this when you say that. I work at the University.

(JANOS demonstrates a dance move. DOMINIQUE and VIOLETTA try it.)

JANOS: I work at the University.

VIOLETTA: I work at the University.

DOMINIQUE: University, University.

JANOS: Where I work is—

DOMINIQUE: The University.

JANOS: Because I work at—

VIOLETTA: The University.

VITO: Aw, please, ya bums.

JANOS: I work at the University.

DOMINIQUE: He means the University of Hog Slaughter.

JANOS: Works for my old man.

VITO: I'm not talking about the yards.

VIOLETTA: Oh no. Not the yards.

VITO: I work at the University.

DOMINIQUE: You keep saying that, what University?

VITO: Okay over there? The Yards. Hogs, Cattle, Sheep, Ducks, stink, stink, stink. Those buildings over there? Professor Bagpipe, Professor Bumpgums think, think. That University of Chicago.

VIOLETTA: And here we are stuck right between.

DOMINIQUE: You work there?

VITO: Yeah, Dominique, I do for another couple of months before I go clobber Hitler.

DOMINIQUE: My hero. Maybe Janos will take me to the Chicago to see Swing Lear.

VIOLETTA: Don't you mean both of us, Nique?

DOMINIQUE: Oh yeah, after Vito gets him a job at the University.

JANOS: You couldn't tell me you got a job? We dropped high school together. We signed up the army together.

VITO: I didn't know where the recruitment was.

JANOS: You're real rugged. Why the big secret, Vito?

VITO: I don't know. It's not like I'm a Professor or anything. I get coffee-and-cake drudging for these science flats.

VIOLETTA: Yeah? And I thought you were teaching advanced jive and panic.

JANOS: Well I need some moolah to spend before I go clobber Hitler too.

VITO: I can ask. That's all I'll say. I can ask.

JANOS: You better, friend.

VITO: Let's work out these moves. We've got a couple months before packing off to fight, and you girls can help us crash the hop.

JANOS: Kopasetic.

VITO: Come on let's jump!

DOMINIQUE: Vito, I don't wanna jump right now. I want to go to the block club meeting.

VITO: What meeting?

DOMINIQUE: You know, the civilian defense meeting.

VIOLETTA: It important to go. Really do something for the war.

VITO: You civilians gonna leave me and Janos to dance without you?

DOMINIQUE: You could come.

VITO: Nique, I promise you—I won't come.

DOMINIQUE: You're some stud, isn't he some stud, Vi?

VIOLETTA: He's a popper right off the cob.

VITO: Hey, I was being sweet. Janos, that's the Bible, right?

JANOS: Sure, boy scout, sweet.

VIOLETTA: Let's go, Dominique. Bye-bye, buy bonds.

VITO: So long Luscious.

(DOMINIQUE *and* VIOLETTA *exit.*)

VITO: I swear I'm going to husk the duchess and have the big moment before I shove off.

JANOS: That's so important.

VITO: I don't want to go into the army without being a man.

JANOS: You could get all the chicks in the world and never be a man.

VITO: Or you could get no chicks and die a square.

(Lights cross fade.)

LEO ON THE PHONE

(Lights rise on LEO *with phone. Distant Geiger)*

*(*ENRICO *works in the shadows with* VITO.*)*

LEO: You know the feeling of walking. One foot in front of the other—the scenery slowly changing—the smell of automobile exhaust the—ürülék—dog ürülék on the sidewalk. Your heart is beating hard on the thought of old curmudgeon Lord Earnest Rutherford of the Cavendish. The illustrious Cavendish at Cambridge where Rutherford hands over the wild mysteries of physical nature like a taxidermist handing over stuffed birds. Rutherford says that searching for energy in atoms is moonshine. Moonshine! How can he say that. He doesn't know.

Rutherford is the past. You think of H G Wells. H G Wells with the great imagination. H G Wells is the future. You think of atoms. You never know what someone else might invent. You're walking. A bus goes by and cars. You are in the present. Many people walking past all bundled up against the chill. It's dreary wet. Thinking Rutherford, Rutherford trapped in facts, and H G Wells open to the future. Science and Imagination. The past and the future, the past and the future, and where are you? Then lightening strikes and you imagine how to make atoms split and split and split and keep splitting in a chain reaction. I know. No, I wasn't in the bathtub when I had this idea, but that is not the point. The point is that I had the idea and now it is reality and there is no going back. Okay. I have to go. I have to go. I love you too.

(LEO *is moving slowly. Walking in memory. Recreating the walk he took when he first imagined the chain reaction.*)

(*Cross fade sound and lights.*)

SCENE: CIVILIAN DEFENSE MEETING

(JANOS *waits outside the civilian defense meeting. Sound of a train rumbling by.* VITO *enters.*)

VITO: Janos?

JANOS: Yeah?

VITO: What are you doin?

JANOS: You know what I'm doin. Waitin.

VITO: Yeah, I hate waitin for our chicks.

JANOS: I just don't know what the hell it's going to be like.

VITO: What?

JANOS: Fighting in the war.

VITO: We've got at least a couple months before we start thinking about that.

JANOS: You never think about it?

VITO: I told you. I'm gonna get Dominique so when I'm sitting in a foxhole in Germany, I'll have something lush to think about.

JANOS: The big moment, that's all you're thinking about?

VITO: Yeah. But not you, right? You got the smarts, right? Your man, H G Wells smarting up your head?

JANOS: I don't know. Yeah.

VITO: Don't you ever get sick of reading and thinking and staring at the wall? You're like the Abercrombiest Abercrombie who ever Abercrombied.

JANOS: What's the opposite of a bomb?

VITO: Abercrombie.

JANOS: Or a bullet.

VITO: Abercrombie.

JANOS: What's the opposite of a bullet.

VITO: I don't know, a kiss?

JANOS: Yeah. But no.

VITO: How different is the war going to be then the yards anyway?

JANOS: I don't want to work in the yards.

VITO: My old man spends his days with a twelve pound hammer smacking hogs and he told me he thinks of some duchess he knew before he married my ma. So I'll kill Nazis all day and think about Dominique.

JANOS: Simple as that.

VITO: Yeah.

JANOS: Vi says it's cold over there. Is it cold over there?

VITO: Will you clam your yap about that, I don't know. I hate waiting. What are they doing in there?

JANOS: Learning how to Save Paper! Save Rubber! Save Rags! And pester your folks to buy Bonds! Uncle Sam loves you Vito.

VITO: Alreet, Uncle, don't get all schmaltzando on me.

JANOS: Vito, no kidding now, how come didn't you tell me about the job?

VITO: I don't know. I guess because it's stupid and really dirty.

JANOS: Really dirty?

VITO: Dirty. Dirty. I get dirty.

JANOS: You're dirty to start with.

VITO: This is dirty above and beyond dirty.

JANOS: Dirtier than being covered in hogs blood?

VITO: Yeah, I work brick slaughter. I cut and haul these heavy bricks of black crap with holes drilled in them.

JANOS: What for?

VITO: For science, stupid.

JANOS: What kind of science is that?

Violetta and Dominique enter from the meeting and pretend they can't see the guys.

DOMINIQUE: Where's our guys, Violetta, do you see our guys? What do they expect, us to wait?

VIOLETTA: Look Dominique there they are! Do you see them?

DOMINIQUE: I do. There they are.

VITO: Real screwball, what'd you learn?

VIOLETTA: Salvage your tin. Here's the pamphlet.

JANOS: *(Reading pamphlet)* Saving Tin is saving lives…

VIOLETTA: There's a movie too, got to see it. Eckhart Hall at the University of Chicago.

DOMINIQUE: Vito's turf.

JANOS: What's the movie?

VIOLETTA: Next of Kin. Here's the pamphlet.

JANOS: *(Reading pamphlet)* Next of Kin directed by Thorold Dickinson.

VIOLETTA: Thor-old? Don't you bet he's a flat?

VITO: Flat and Brit as a board. What else?

JANOS: 1941. Drama. Duration: one hour, thirty-five minutes. Starring Mervyn Johns as number 23, and

John Chandos as number 16. Also starring Nova
Pilbeam as Beppie Leemans.

VIOLETTA: Nova Pilbeam!

DOMINIQUE: As Beppie Leemans?

JANOS: And Brefni O'Rorke as the Brigadier. Ever hear
of any of them?

DOMINIQUE: You kidding, I keep swooney Brefni
O'Rorke under my pillow.

VIOLETTA: Next to Cary Grant? What's he think about
that?

DOMINIQUE: Nothing, I keep Cary in my heart.

VIOLETTA: Swooney.

VITO: Sure. What's the civilian defense angle?

JANOS: "Be like Dad, keep Mum—careless talk costs
lives!" A woman is chatting to her friend about her son
who is in the war serving as a Commando in one of
the elite raiding groups. Her conversation is overheard
by a Fifth Columnist. The information is passed along
the network of traitors and sleeper agents so when
the Commando team strikes, the German defenses are
ready for them.
Undoubtedly Hitler's lightning conquest of Europe
was aided by the "Fifth Column". Is there a Fifth
Column in your neighborhood?

(JANOS, VIOLETTA, DOMINIQUE *consider for a beat and
then turn to* VITO.)

DOMINIQUE: Are you part of the Fifth Column?

VITO: I'm a big wheel in the fifth column.

DOMINIQUE: It's not a joke. How would I know? All of
a sudden you work for the "University".

VITO: Are you kidding me?

DOMINIQUE: No. All of sudden you have money and you work for the University. Doesn't anyone else think that's suspicious? Our friend Vito here, WORKING. You hate work.

VITO: Oh come on, Doll, you know I love the cabbage.

VIOLETTA: Yeah, and you didn't come to the defense meeting.

VITO: Neither did Janos.

DOMINIQUE: Janos didn't go to Swing Lear.

VITO: You think I'm a spy cause I went to Swing Lear?

DOMINIQUE: I don't know. Are you?

VITO: I spy your juicy lips and your—

DOMINIQUE: I'm not kidding.

VITO: Alreet. I'm going to get Janos a job at the University, then you can think he's a spy too.

VIOLETTA: I'm going to the movie.

JANOS: *Next of Kin*?

DOMINIQUE: Yeah. Me too. You know, I feel a patriotic choke coming on.

VITO: Alreet, let's go.

DOMINIQUE: What. Now you're going to come?

VITO: Not a chance, Nique. I'm gonna get our boy Janos a job at the University.

JANOS: Bout time.

VIOLETTA: Nique—to the flick.

DOMINIQUE: I'm coming.

(Lights fade. Sound of movie, newsreel. collage—time marches on type thing.)

SCENE: PLUTO'S WORKSHOP

(Sound of Geiger counter. Lights up on ENRICO *measuring graphite, cutting it with a saw, and drilling it on a press.)*

*(*JANOS *and* VITO *wait for* ENRICO *to tell them what to do.)*

*(*LEO *visible working in his office.)*

JANOS: Vito.

VITO: Yeah?

JANOS: Remember what you used to say?

VITO: Nah.

JANOS: I work at the University.

VITO: So?

JANOS: We work at the University.

VITO: Ain't that the Bible.

JANOS: Three months at—

VITO: The University.

JANOS: Real dirty work at—

VITO: The University.

JANOS: Three months ago I thought you were just big talk.

VITO: Now you know—I'm big walk.

JANOS: Yeah. In case I never thanked you, thanks for the drudge.

VITO: Reet, Schmaltzando Joe.

(Cross fade to Responsibility scene)

SCENE: RESPONSIBILITY

(Lights rise on DOMINIQUE, VIOLETTA. JANOS *and* VITO *are visible in the lab with* ENRICO.*)*

VIOLETTA: When I line up all the really hard things about life?, waiting takes the cake.

DOMINIQUE: We don't have to wait. Vito and Janos will find us.

VIOLETTA: I want to wait, that's what makes it so awful.

*(*LAURA *encounters* DOMINIQUE *and* VIOLETTA.*)*

DOMINIQUE: Hello Missus.

VIOLETTA: You look cold.

LAURA: You are those kids.

VIOLETTA: We are?

DOMINIQUE: What kids?

LAURA: Those kids who dance with my husband.

VIOLETTA: Your husband is enthusiastic, isn't he?

(Cross fade to Pluto's Workshop)

PLUTO'S WORKSHOP

JANOS: Vito? My papers came through so I'm going to boot camp next week.

VITO: Yeah? Me too.

JANOS: Yeah?

VITO: Yeah.

JANOS: Were you going to tell me?

VITO: I just did.

(Cross fade to Responsibility scene)

RESPONSIBILITY

VIOLETTA: How long you been married to the Professor?

LAURA: Eight years.

DOMINIQUE: What's it like, eight years of the same dish?

LAURA: Fascinating.

DOMINIQUE: Fascinating or not, eight years is a long time.

VIOLETTA: Your folks have been married for decades, Nique.

DOMINIQUE: Yeah, look at the aggrevation—what do you do, Mrs, when he just drives you nuts?

LAURA: Drives me nuts?

(Cross fade to Pluto's scene)

PLUTO'S

JANOS: You hear that Professor, both of us are going into the army next week.

ENRICO: Is that so? Next week.

JANOS: Yeah, Professor, and in case I never thanked you, thanks for the drudge.

ENRICO: Boys, what makes me happy?

VITO/JANOS: Drudge!

ENRICO: Drudge is right.

(Cross fade to Responsibility scene)

RESPONSIBILITY

VIOLETTA: Yeah, what do you do when your guy stinks or says things that make your blood boil or gives you the cold shoulder.

DOMINIQUE: That's my old man. Silent treatment. Real icy.

LAURA: Yes, I don't know what to do.

VIOLETTA: Oh.

DOMINIQUE: Oh. He's driving you nuts right now, huh?

LAURA: Yes.

VIOLETTA: Does he know he's driving you nuts?

LAURA: Yes.

DOMINIQUE: What's he doing?

LAURA: He's scaring me.

VIOLETTA: Yeah?

LAURA: Yes.

DOMINIQUE: I know what that's like. Did you see that movie, Next of Kin?

LAURA: Of course.

DOMINIQUE: So now my guy has money, and swears he works at the University, but the thing is Mrs., he's not the industrious type.

LAURA: Does he say what he does at the University?

DOMINIQUE: No.

LAURA: My husband can't tell me what he does either.

(Cross fade to Pluto's Workshop)

PLUTO'S

ENRICO: Get into the world with your hands, and with
your head. You boys have been working hard with
your hands today, now here's a question so you can
work hard with your head—

VITO: How thick can the dust get on a window before
it starts to fall off? Then you got to ask what window?
What kind of dust? What time a day? What the hell!
Your questions just make more questions, Professor,
and my head still hurts from the last one you asked.

ENRICO: That means it's working, Vito.

JANOS: Shoot, Professor.

ENRICO: The Fermi question for the day is: how fast can
you boys work and still be precise?

JANOS: Fast and precise?

ENRICO: You're only here another week, so don't think
about it too long. Here, this block is ready. Take it to
the Hundred Acre Wood.

VITO: Hundred Acre Wood and fast.

JANOS: And precise.

(JANOS *and* VITO *grab the block of graphite and begin to
move it when they slip and drop it. They laugh.*)

ENRICO: Vito! Janos!

VITO: Slippery stuff, Professor.

ENRICO: What kind of bricks are these? How tightly are
they fitting next to each other? How precisely are they
cut? How precisely are they measured? Do these bricks
have a tolerance for being dropped?

JANOS: We just slipped, Doctor Fermi.

ENRICO: You can't slip. Get it? Now I have to cut this
one all over, and that will put us behind. We're in a

delicate race, boys. You need to put on the gas and be precise. You can handle it or not?

JANOS: Sure, Professor. Gas and precise.

VITO: What's this stuff called again?

ENRICO: Have you read Winnie the Pooh?

VITO: No.

JANOS: Piglet.

VITO: Piglet! Is slippery. Put this on the dance floor and I'd be a hot hose in flying kicks. Check this move, I call it the Piglet Jump. *(He does a preposterous spin.)*

ENRICO: Next week jump, right now engage the clutch! Junk that block, I'll cut another. *(He goes back to measuring.)*

JANOS: Sorry, Professor. I guess these three months of hauling and stacking blocks of Piglet and trying to answer your questions have been getting to us.

ENRICO: Push yourselves, boys.

JANOS: Sorry, Professor.

VITO: Reet, Janos, lend a mitt.

(JANOS helps pick up the graphite block and they walk out of earshot.)

JANOS: Don't you ever wonder what all this is for? An old squash court stacked to the ceiling with fifty-seven layers of "Piglet" and "Tigger"?

VITO: No.

JANOS: I do.

VITO: Just don't let it slow you down.

JANOS: You ever talk to him talk to him?

VITO: Yeah, how I got the job was I was walking 57th and caught a backcap in my flops. It was domestic between the Professor and his old lady. She doesn't like it here, he does. He was standing on his work and she was hung up about it.

JANOS: So you are a spy.

VITO: What! No, dig, I just overheard. When she left, him and me bumped gums about it. And the next couple of days he looked me up and hired me.

JANOS: Did you overhear anything about what we're doing here?

VITO: No, and stop it with the spy questions already.

JANOS: I'm curious is all. Ever wonder why the Professor and the rest of them come to work in suits, change into coveralls, and then at the end of the day, shower and change back into suits?

VITO: The Piglet craps up the coveralls.

JANOS: Ever wonder why all the machines and stuff have names from Winnie the Pooh?

VITO: I don't know. The Professor has two little bambinos at home?

JANOS: Okay Eeyore, ever notice the armed guards at the door we pass everyday?

VITO: Now you're scaring me you gammin fifth columnist. Just shut up and sing.

JANOS: What? Sing what?

VITO: Something American. Dinah won't you blow. (*Calling to* ENRICO) Song time, Professor, you know Dinah won't you blow?

ENRICO: I don't.

VITO: We'll teach you.

(VITO *feeds* ENRICO *the lines. The three begin to sing.*)

VITO/JANOS/ENRICO: (*Singing*)
We been drudgin' in the squash court,

All the live long day.
We been drudgin' in the squash court,
Just to pass the time away.
Don't you hear the whistle blowing?
Rise up so early in the morn.
Don't you hear the Professor shouting
"Dinah, blow your horn?"
Dinah, won't you blow,
Dinah, won't you blow,
Dinah, won't you blow your horn?
Dinah, won't you blow,
Dinah, won't you blow,
Dinah, won't you blow your horn?

Someone's in the kitchen with Dinah.
Someone's in the kitchen, I know.
Someone's in the kitchen with Dinah
Strumming on the old banjo.
Fee, fie, fiddle-e-i-o.
Fee, fie, fiddle-e-i-o-o-o-o.
Fee, fie, fiddle-e-i-o.
Strumming on the old banjo.

(Lights cross fade to Responsibility scene)

RESPONSIBILITY

VIOLETTA: So, Mrs, your husband works at "the University" and can't tell you what he does—you think your husband is part of the fifth column?

LAURA: No. No. Not that. I think something worse.

VIOLETTA: What's worse than being a traitor?

LAURA: We all have a responsibility to our country, yes, but we also have a responsibility to ourselves and the whole world. We're citizens of the world.

DOMINIQUE: I don't get you.

LAURA: What is our deepest responsibility?

DOMINIQUE: …Not to get knocked up?

VIOLETTA: Nique!

DOMINIQUE: I don't know—what are you saying?

LAURA: There is a war. You say okay, 'I'm against killing, but there is a war.'

VIOLETTA: You're against killing?

LAURA: Oh yes, I don't believe in it.

DOMINIQUE: You got to kill Hitler. Don't you?

VIOLETTA: I think so, don't you?

LAURA: What if you just kill Hitler, Mussolini, Hirohito? Will all the fascists just go away?

DOMINIQUE: I don't know, maybe.

LAURA: Maybe you have to kill all the fascists? And where do fascists come from? Do you have to kill everyone in the whole country? Do you have to kill the whole country?

VIOLETTA: That question is out of my depth.

DOMINIQUE: Mrs, you can't kill a whole country.

LAURA: What if you can. What if you can kill all of Germany or Japan or Italy?

VIOLETTA: You're scary, you know that?

DOMINIQUE: I think she's one of those nervous ladies.

LAURA: No, I'm not one of those nervous ladies.

DOMINIQUE: You talk like one.

VIOLETTA: Yeah, scary.

LAURA: The world is scary and I want to change that, but I don't know what to do.

VIOLETTA: We know what to do and, I've got some pamphlets that are pretty clear about what there is to do. Maybe you want one.

DOMINIQUE: Yeah, Mrs, you should come to the civilian defense meetings with us. We learn so much. It's uh, uh, fascinating.

VIOLETTA: The whole country is a team and each city and neighborhood and even every single household has to do their part for the team.

DOMINIQUE: We have to keep up the pull at home while our boys are fighting.

VIOLETTA: That's exactly what we have to do.

DOMINIQUE: That's our responsibility. Come on Vi.

VIOLETTA: Mrs. isn't it clear what you have to do? If you're a citizen.

DOMINIQUE: Let's go, Vi.

LAURA: I wish it was clear what I have to do. Do you really believe that a pamphlet or a meeting makes you a citizen?

VIOLETTA: If you're an American.

DOMINIQUE: Bye-bye Vi.

VIOLETTA: I'm coming.

(DOMINIQUE *and* VIOLETTA *exit.* LAURA *stays.*)

(*Black out. Time passes. Geiger counter sound collage.*)

LEO ON THE PHONE

(Lights rise on LEO *with phone.)*

*(*ENRICO *and the boys work in the shadows just beyond* LEO.*)*

LEO: We have done tests. We have done many tests. Fermi is a testing madman. Reference tests. Control tests. He's made model after model and working minatures. But can we be sure? We can't. The numbers of course are unerring, but what are numbers against the real world? When the time comes for the reaction to happen, and that time is fast approaching, then I will eat two dinners, two breakfests, two lunches because atoms will split and split and split and who knows if they'll ever stop.

*(*LAURA *enters.* LEO *is shocked.)*

LEO: I have to go. Me too. Me too. Me too. Me too. Alright, I love you. Goodbye. Don't tell anyone we talked. *(He hangs up the phone.)* I imagine you overheard me.

LAURA: Yes.

LEO: This is a top secret facility, Laura. The very top of secrecy.

LAURA: Does the person you were talking to know that?

LEO: I was talking to…Einstein.

LAURA: You love Albert Einstein?

LEO: Doesn't everyone? Love Albert Einstein? How did you get past the guards?

LAURA: Those two nice helpful young men were guards?

LEO: Not after this. Laura, what are you doing here?

LAURA: I want to talk.

LEO: Talk?

LAURA: Yes. I can't talk to Enrico, right? So I will talk to you.

LEO: I am listening.

LAURA: Leo, my heart hurts like the sky before a storm.

LEO: Because Enrico goes dancing with those kids from the corner?

LAURA: What? No. Listen to me.

LEO: I know the last three months have been hard and the last three nights he's only come home to brush his teeth—we have been working late.

LAURA: That's not it, Leo, I can live with feeling lonely.

LEO: We are in a race to win a War. Anything Enrico has to do to get by. The magnitude of what we are doing is bigger than your marriage, or your family. I'm sure you know that.

LAURA: You're not listening to me! Listen to me!

LEO: Alright. Talk.

LAURA: The secrecy around what you are doing, you and Enrico, makes me suspicious.

LEO: Suspicious?

LAURA: You don't race to win a war by working in secret on diplomacy, do you Leo?

LEO: It's a race—

LAURA: I know. To win the war, but I want to understand what it means to 'win the war.' To win the war? What does that mean?

LEO: What if it means the end of fascism?

LAURA: The work you are doing will end the idea of fascism? There will always be fascists. You can't end an idea, can you?

LEO: I don't know, Laura.

LAURA: You do know. Unless you are inventing something that will make the whole world all at once forget.

LEO: We're not.

LAURA: So if you can't end an idea, how do you change it? With a weapon? If we win the war because of a new weapon, are fascists really going to become more reasonable, more sane?

LEO: Laura, an idea has come along that has already changed every other idea that has come after it.

LAURA: The big secret?

LEO: It is a horrifying idea that has changed everything. But it may be less horrifying than Hitler taking over the world.

LAURA: You don't know?

LEO: No. But it is a risk we must now take.

LAURA: What does Enrico think?

LEO: I envy Enrico, his conscience is clear. He is inspired by the work before him. To him it is pure science.

LAURA: How do you know? Do you know his mind?

LEO: Oh. No, you're right, I don't.

LAURA: Know your own mind.

LEO: I do. I spend all my time in it.

LAURA: Maybe you should spend less time in it if you find horrifying ideas in there.

LEO: My conscience is not clear, Laura, believe me. But the Government owns this idea of mine—I gave them the patent because it scared me to imagine Hitler with it. And the work is nearly complete, and the momentum will absolutely carry it through. My conscience doesn't matter now.

LAURA: It always matters Leo.

LEO: Do you think that is true?

LAURA: Yes.

LEO: I am still afraid of Hitler.

LAURA: And after Hitler?

LEO: We will see.

LAURA: Wait and see? Leo, it would be shameful to win the war, but lose the peace that follows.

LEO: I think that you are talking about treason.

LAURA: I don't know. What is treason like? I have to do something.

LEO: Maybe you should talk to Enrico.

LAURA: Did you know that by using only his thumb and forefinger, Enrico can measure the speed, altitude and distance of a passing cloud.

LEO: It doesn't surprise me.

LAURA: He loves things like that. He loves questions that make more questions. Now I'm asking, Leo, how far do you go to win a war?

LEO: I don't know.

LAURA: But does it make you a traitor to wonder? *(She exits.)*

(JANOS and VITO and ENRICO are in coveralls, working.)

(Momentum of sound picks up.)

(Lights cross fade.)

SCENE: MEETING WITH LEO

(Lights rise on LEO *outside* ARTHUR's *house at night.* LEO *throws pebbles at the window until* ARTHUR *comes out.)*

LEO: Arthur. Arthur. Come out. Come out Arthur.

ARTHUR: *(Exiting his house with a coat wrapped around his pajamas)* Is it happening? Is it time? Has the Italian Navigator landed in the new world?

LEO: No. It's not happening. I just need to talk.

ARTHUR: Leo, calling me out of my home at this hour of the night—you really are an abrasive creature.

LEO: Is that better than being an asshole?

ARTHUR: No, it's not.

LEO: Arthur, I have been an asshole.

ARTHUR: Well.

LEO: I need to talk to you about grave concerns.

ARTHUR: Your salary again? I've already told you—

LEO: Not my salary. Though sixty-six hundred dollars a year is hardly proper compensation for a bunion let alone an asshole. The issue I wish to bring to your attention once again is secrecy.

ARTHUR: You know what is strange, Leo, you're constantly harping on secrecy. And yet, I am constantly defending you to the government because they believe that you're security risk number one.

LEO: Arthur, I may have breeched security.

ARTHUR: Certainly. What?!

LEO: I have been on the phone trying to untangle my conscience, and then, today, Laura Fermi stopped in my office—

ARTHUR: Leo. There is a new top man named Leslie R. Groves. He is a general, a West Pointer.

LEO: You're not top man anymore?

ARTHUR: Groves has taken over the Manhattan Project—that's what this whole operation is now called.

LEO: How cosmopolitan.

ARTHUR: Listen. Groves is not a trifler. All the materials are being procured through the Manhattan Engineering District—to throw off spies.

LEO: It is amazing. Amazing.

ARTHUR: What?

LEO: You're out walking one night, and you're about to cross the street and you're angry thinking about pompous scientists who hold on to the past and you're thinking about the future, striving to show up those old goats, and a simple idea occurs to you. What an idea, you think! And maybe because you're out on the street and there are people all around you, you debate with your conscience—should you keep the idea to yourself?
Is this idea too dangerous to let loose? Anger and secrecy, Arthur, pathetic inspirations.

ARTHUR: You're scaring me and I have no idea what you're talking about.

LEO: I'm talking about getting Einstein to write a letter to President Roosevelt.

ARTHUR: Saying what?

LEO: Saying that we can not keep the Manhattan Project a secret anymore. We must tell everyone. Our allies first, but then even our enemies—

ARTHUR: We're at war, you understand? You're not an American citizen. Your visa is from Hungary. Where's that? You have been pathologically secretive, now you're telling me you may have breeched security, and you want to write a letter revealing the secrets of the Manhattan Project? Groves has already threatened to have you jailed.

LEO: It will bring disaster upon the world if we win the war, but lose the peace that will follow.

ARTHUR: I don't want to hear this. You are not saying this.

LEO: I am saying this and I mean it. What separates us, Arthur, is that I answer only to my conscience.

ARTHUR: Treason is punishable by death, Leo. I think. Yes. I can't talk to you anymore. Leo, I've enjoyed working with you these last few months. But. Goodnight. Be careful my friend.

(ARTHUR *exits.* JANOS *enters cautiously.*)

JANOS: Troubles, Professor?

LEO: What? Who are you?

JANOS: I work at the Thoughtful Place. You know, on the Hundred Acre Wood and all that.

LEO: Yes, yes.

JANOS: Janos. Miklos.

LEO: Hungarian?

JANOS: My family is. From near Tatabanya. I was born in Chicago.

LEO: I was born in Budapest.

JANOS: I've heard of it.

LEO: I hope you have.

JANOS: Can I ask you something, Doctor Szilard?

LEO: I'm preoccupied right now. If you don't mind half an answer.

JANOS: We've been perculating round the clock like crazy down there, and I want to know, what are we building?

LEO: What?

JANOS: In the squash court with the Piglet, the Tigger—

LEO: STOP. STOP. Is this a joke?

JANOS: No. A joke?

LEO: A sick test of my loyalty?

JANOS: No, I, I heard you talking, and I—

LEO: You OVERHEARD me talking?

JANOS: Don't blow your wig, Professor. I'm curious is all. See I read this book called *World Set Free* by H G Wells. Ever heard of it?

(LEO *steps back to observe* JANOS.)

LEO: Are you a spy? You are a spy?

JANOS: You're wacky, know that?

LEO: Who is your boss? Take me to him.

JANOS: I thought you were my boss. One of them, and Professor Fermi is the other.

LEO: Fermi sent you?

JANOS: No. No one sent me. I just came from the Thoughtful Place. But I'm making tracks now, bye-bye, buy bonds.

LEO: No. Stay right here. You say you read *World Set Free*, and you wondered what we were building. What is the connection?

JANOS: What?

LEO: The connection in your mind between World Set Free and the squash court.

JANOS: Tigger—uranium. The book talks about radio-
activity and uranium and carolinium and then I read
that newspaper article about the atom being split
and that was uranium too. So. I don't know. I'm just
curious. If you don't want to talk about it, at least tell
me why we call it Tigger.

LEO: I don't know how to take you. What's your name
again?

JANOS: Janos.

LEO: Where do you live?

JANOS: Back of the Yards. 52nd and Ashland. Want to
talk to my mom?

LEO: And you..why do you want to know what we're
doing?

JANOS: I'm curious that way, I like to think.

LEO: What do you think we're doing down there?

JANOS: I don't know, but I'm going into the army soon,
and so, you know, I've been thinking a lot lately. You
know in World Set Free how they had atomic bombs?
I was wondering why someone couldn't invent the
opposite of the atomic bomb.

LEO: What would the opposite of the atomic bomb be?

JANOS: I don't know. Maybe something that instead of
blowing things apart and burning forever, pulls things
together.

LEO: An attractive force.

JANOS: Yeah, like a gigantic magnet.

LEO: Tell me more about your idea.

JANOS: Well, I'm going into the army, right, and I was
thinking about sitting in a foxhole and bombs are
dropping around me and I imagined getting hit by a
bomb and blown to pieces. So I'd be laying there in

bloody pieces and wouldn't it be nice if a medic or someone came along and dropped a thing on me that would pull all my pieces back together.

LEO: That would be miraculous.

JANOS: Or something got dropped on a whole battlefield that put everyone back together. But I know it's impossible.

LEO: You never know what someone else might invent. Do you like H G Wells?

JANOS: You shred it wheat. All his books. *The Time Machine, Invisible Man, War of the Worlds, Island of Doctor Moreau.*

LEO: I know Wells.

JANOS: Know him, know him?

LEO: We're friends.

JANOS: Yeah? Friends with H G Wells, Perfection! What's he like? Can you talk to him?

LEO: We talk.

JANOS: What's his next book?

LEO: He's kind of stuck, he told me.

JANOS: How come?

LEO: He says that human history becomes more and more a race between education and catastrophe. He's not sure how to write about that.

JANOS: Do you think it's true?

LEO: He's a smart man.

JANOS: So the opposite of education is catastrophe?

LEO: Yes, but…

JANOS: Does he mean education like books?

LEO: Education like potential energy. Maybe education is your opposite bomb.

JANOS: Bombs are the opposite of education?

LEO: I think so.

JANOS: So when I get hit by a bomb and scattered in tiny pieces, reading a book is going to pull me together?

LEO: Well…

JANOS: How good a book would that have to be?

LEO: I'm talking about the kind of education that energizes you.

JANOS: Hitler seems pretty energetic to me, and no matter how educated I am, he's still the one dropping the bombs on me.

LEO: Yes, but if the German people were truly educated. Energetically educated. If the entire world was energetically educated. If people pursued knowledge of all of human culture with the same passion that Hitler is pursuing conquest of it, then he would never have come to power.

JANOS: Get working on that H G Wells time machine to go back before Hitler and take us to school, Professor.

LEO: Or. All you have to do is have the idea. That's the way the universe works. Put the idea into your imagination and let it go forward. We're inventing the future right now. That's the true time machine. We say right now that there is something out there opposite of the atomic bomb, that balances the atomic bomb. We say that and it's going to happen. We each tell our friends, and they tell their friends and somebody has an idea, and another person adds to that idea and this is how the Universe works, the idea comes to be. The two of us are inventing the future right now.

JANOS: Should I tell my mom?

LEO: Tell your mom. *(He exits in a hurry.)*

JANOS: Are you going to tell your mom? Professor? Could I tell H G Wells? Professor?

(Blackout. Sound of Geiger counter.)

PLUTO'S WORKSHOP THE BIG EVENT

(Lights rise on ENRICO *tweaking instruments.* JANOS *and* VITO *stand by with buckets. Geiger counter ticks arrhythmically.)*

ENRICO: Look at this.

ENRICO: Do you see?

VITO: No. What?

*(*JANOS *and* VITO *look.)*

ENRICO: Good numbers. Good numbers. Hard work, strong focus, and numbers that jive with months of calculation. You can feel it in your hands, and in your head. The Hundred Acre Wood has grown to maturity and once we prune the safety branches, the Hunny will flow. Congratulations Gentlemen.

VITO: Professor, I'm no gentleman—

ENRICO: I mean she's ready, boys. When Arthur and Szilard arrive we'll start. Grab the buckets.

JANOS: What do we do with these?

ENRICO: With those you be careful and don't spill a drop. That's Kanga and that's Roo. They're gonna douse the sting if we get attacked by bees when the Hunny starts to flow. But I'm not worried about sting. No, not at all. Good numbers.

VITO: Reet and smooth.

JANOS: Whose got Kanga and whose got Roo?

ENRICO: Doesn't matter. Climb to the top of the Hundred Acre Wood and stand ready. We're going to prune the branches slowly, a couple of inches at a time. I'll watch the numbers. We won't have to, but if we have to, I'll tell you when to pour. But boys, the Hundred Acre Wood is very delicate and even a drop, a single drop of Kanga or Roo could ruin this batch of Hunny, so be precise.

JANOS: Okay, Professor, precise. Science is so different than I thought it would be.

ENRICO: What did you think?

JANOS: I don't know, but I never thought I'd be in a squash court with a bucket of Kanga or Roo ready to dump it on something that looks like a giant black birthday cake and is called the Hundred Acre Wood, and I never thought you could invent the future by having a single idea.

ENRICO: Our work here in the Thoughtful Place can hardly be reduced to a single idea. We are about to open the door on a great new future.

JANOS: I wasn't talking about the Thoughtful Place, I was talking about the opposite of the atomic bomb. That future.

ENRICO: *(Tightening)* Stop. The atomic bomb?

VITO: Atomic bomb?

JANOS: Yeah. All we have to do is tell everyone about the opposite of the atomic bomb, and the idea will leap from one mind to another until it's perfection. That's what Doctor Szilard says anyway.

ENRICO: SZILARD TOLD YOU ABOUT THE ATOMIC BOMB?!

JANOS: No, H G Wells did in *World Set Free*. But Doctor Szilard is friends with H G Wells.

ENRICO: You were talking to Szilard about atomic bombs?

JANOS: We were talking about the opposite of atomic bombs.

VITO: That kills as the name for a dance move, the atomic bomb. *(He moves.)*

ENRICO: Stop it. This isn't funny. I said stop it!

VITO: Sorry—

(ARTHUR enters from stage left in coveralls.)

ARTHUR: Good afternoon everyone. Today is the big day. Are you as excited as I am, Enrico?

ENRICO: No Arthur, Janos says he and Szilard invented the future last night—the opposite of the atomic bomb!

ARTHUR: Well. How contrary.

ENRICO: Contrary for the master of secrecy, the INVENTOR of secrecy to be talking to teenagers about the atomic bomb.

JANOS: The opposite of the atomic bomb.

ENRICO: It's a long step from this reactor to the atomic bomb, but from here to the opposite, I can't—did you calculate how this opposite might work?

JANOS: It's just an idea, Doctor Fermi, an idea.

(LEO enters in overalls.)

ENRICO: Szilard! Janos told us about your opposite atomic bomb. What a fascinating idea. What a surprise. What an invention. Of course we haven't even quite achieved the chain reaction yet, but no matter. No matter. Ideas are easy. Ideas are abundant. Did you think how to get to your high-minded opposite from our humble work down here?

LEO: I did. I wrote to Einstein about it.

ARTHUR: I'd better not hear this.

LEO: A monumental letter. One of my best, I think.

ARTHUR: Who will change the subject?

LEO: The opposite of the atomic bomb will work by the very act of talking about it and thinking about it.

ENRICO: You must be insane. Really. I'm beside myself.

ARTHUR: I will change the subject. Hallelujah, Enrico. Look at this progress. Amazing. How big is the Hundred Acre Wood?

ENRICO: Forty tons of Tigger oxide, six tons of Tigger metal, and three hundred eighty-five tons of Piglet.

LEO: The Hundred Acre Wood. Doesn't the fact that we're calling the first nuclear chain reactor, "the Hundred Acre Wood" scare the crap out of anyone else?

ENRICO: Arthur! You are hearing this!

ARTHUR: Ah, no. Yes. Not willingly.

LEO: The mystery and grandeur and horrific danger of the atom hidden behind the names from a children's book?

ENRICO: Have you ever read Winnie-the-Pooh?

LEO: No.

ENRICO: It's not just a children's book! It is also grand and mysterious and dangerous.

ARTHUR: So. My. What a remarkable pile.

LEO: Again, pile? Pile makes the reactor sound like dog urulek.

ENRICO: No name can diminish the new order of magnitude we are creating here.

LEO: It is a new order of magnitude entirely to set loose the atom on an unsuspecting world.

ENRICO: Either we achieve the bomb first, or Hitler does, to quote a man I once knew named Leo Szilard.

LEO: Welcome to Pluto's workshop, I am Enrico Fermi's scientist within. Numbers, numbers. Numbers are all I see and all that matters!

ENRICO: Well, I am Leo Szilard's imagination. I jump from point A to point D and wonder why you're wasting your time with B and C—

LEO: For Enrico Fermi, what is point D? He can't see it, it must be—a figment, a mirage—

ENRICO: For Leo Szilard top secrecy means top hypocracy—talking to teenagers—

LEO: At least I'm not dancing with them, like the Italian Navigator!

ENRICO: Oh, no, no, not dancing, with teenagers the Hungarian is inventing the future!

LEO: Someone better start inventing it, because this reactor can only mean destruction—

ENRICO: And Fascists are great humanitarians!

LEO: Of course I know why we're pursuing the bomb, now I think it's time to imagine what will follow.

ENRICO: If our work is compromised because atomic secrets leap from mind to mind, what will follow is losing the war!

LEO: Secrecy is now more dangerous than the bomb itself.

ENRICO: (*Simultaneous with* LEO) *Che cosa! Siete insani voi siete invisibili un fantasma un niente e tutto l'improvviso vi transforme in un monumento al* lunacy!

LEO: *(Simultaneous with* ENRICO*)* I imagined the chain reaction which will lead to the atomic bomb, and I can't help that, but now it is time to imagine the future. I don't believe in secrecy anymore.

ENRICO: I don't care what you believe in or don't. The work we are doing here is TOP SECRET. The very top of secrecy! A rare place to be! It is a privilege to be here! Right Arthur?!

ARTHUR: A moment ago, suspicion. Now, certainty. I am in Hell.

*(*ENRICO *and* LEO *are in a face off.* ARTHUR *is ineffectual. Geiger counter ticks.)*

(Beat. Sound of Geiger picks up speed.)

ENRICO: Do you hear that? That sound is the sound of a miracle.

*(*ENRICO *draws out the control rod again and the Geiger picks up.)*

ENRICO: Listen.

(The Geiger counter roars. Everyone turns.)

ENRICO: You hear that? The Hundred Acre Wood is self-sustaining. She's critical. Do you hear that? The energy is flowing. Energy for houses, boats, airplanes, even cars—why not energy for cars? Tell me she's not beautiful. Tell me she's not useful.

ARTHUR: The Italian Navigator has landed in the new world.

LEO: Let us hope that the natives are peaceful.

ARTHUR: Yes. And well behaved.

(The Geiger roars.)

ENRICO: The first sustained nuclear chain reaction. December 2nd, 1942.

(Lights fade. sound of Geiger rolls into sounds of city.)

THE NAVIGATOR HAS LANDED

(Lights rise as LEO *enters downstage right with his phone. Everyone else enters upstage right. They are at a party at* ENRICO *and* LAURA's *house. They are joyful. Swing music slowly rises. They begin to dance.)*

LEO: *(On phone)* I am. I am. Yes. I'm angry. I wish that I had imagined something completely different. So different and simple that people around the world would be smacking their foreheads in wonder. An attractive, creative force so powerful that even if Hitler had an atomic bomb, he would wilt from frustration. I don't know. I don't know. Maybe it would be like a golden wave sweeping across the entire globe—setting things in order. Of course I know it sounds ridiculous. I know that.

No. Don't tease. I'm not afraid to imagine such a thing can exist. In the meantime, think about it. Talk to your friends about it. Yeah. Talk. The pump is not doing well, too noisy, thanks for asking. I have to go. Me too. I'll see you soon. I love you. Goodbye.

*(*LEO *exits and reenters with his suitcase. He watches as* LAURA *approaches* ENRICO.*)*

LAURA: Everyone is congratulating you. You must be proud.

ENRICO: Yes.

LAURA: Tell me what you have achieved.

ENRICO: A miracle Laura.

LAURA: What kind of miracle?

ENRICO: A nuclear chain reaction requires an exact alignment of many different factors. Uranium. Uranium is pure beauty, Laura. It gives off neutrons, neutrons like tiny spots of light, like tiny pearls flying in all directions—moving invisibly through the world.

Traveling through the air, through the earth, through our bodies. Picture it, a ball of Uranium shedding pearls like a firework that never stops—and if you have enough Uranium arranged in calculated rows, when a single neutron travels out from one uranium atom and is absorbed by another, two are emitted, those two can easily reach two more. And those can reach 4 and those 8 and 16 and 32 and 64 and soon billions and billions of atoms are splitting and releasing energy. Energy.

(ENRICO *takes* LAURA *in his arms to dance.*)

LAURA: Energy Enrico? For what?

ENRICO: For cars, boats, airplanes, even for houses Laura can you imagine—

LAURA: What else?

ENRICO: The sky will be the limit.

LAURA: Don't tell me that.

ENRICO: What should I tell you?

LAURA: Tell me something ridiculous like the length to which icicles grow or the altitude of a cloud floating by. Or talk to me about our children because tenderness rarely stands a chance in history, does it Enrico?

(ENRICO *tries to embrace* LAURA, *but she turns away softly.* VITO *dances with* DOMINIQUE, JANOS *with* VIOLETTA.)

VITO: Dominique. Please? Please? Please? Please?

DOMINIQUE: You learn a new word?

VITO: Yeah. Please. Ever hear of it? Please. I'm leaving to fight Hitler tomorrow. Please? Please?

VIOLETTA: Vito. You got to sneak that word up on her, not hit her over the head with it. I bet it would work if you were real swooney and Fred Astaired her over to a corner to talk about sugar rations, and butter. Talk

about the movies, Brefni O'Rouke and Cary Grant.
Talk about Cab Calloway and Benny Goodman. Then
gently pull her to you, and put your hand soft on her
knee—don't go for the mush, but look her in the eyes
and ask please.

JANOS: That goes for you?

VIOLETTA: We could try it.

LEO: Janos.

(LEO *motions* JANOS *over.*)

JANOS: *(To* VIOLETTA*)* Don't go anywhere. *(To* LEO*)*
Professor?

LEO: We've achieved the unbelievable, Janos, so you've
got to promise me something.

JANOS: I don't know if I can, you know me and Vito are
shipping out tomorrow, and tonight goes by the name
Violetta.

LEO: I still want you to promise.

JANOS: Alreet, what?

LEO: Promise that you'll always be thinking of the
incredible, unbelievable thing that is the opposite of
the atomic bomb.

JANOS: Alreet, but it might be hard to think of if I'm
preoccupied.

LEO: Alright, maybe not tonight, but tomorrow and the
next day and-

JANOS: It might be hard to think of it if I'm cold too.

LEO: Cold?

JANOS: I'm afraid of being cold when I get over there. Is
it cold over there?

LEO: You should think of it most when you're afraid.
And if I die before I think of this thing, and you die

before you think of it, then I want you to promise that you'll make your children think of it.

JANOS: Children?! Don't get ahead of me, Professor.

LEO: When you get back from the war, I'm going to introduce you to H G Wells.

JANOS: Perfection!

LEO: He would agree, now more then ever, imagination is the true work of our lives.

JANOS: So long, Professor.

LEO: So long Janos, stay warm.

(LEO *exits.* JANOS *finds a corner with* VIOLETTA. *Music rises. The party swings.*)

(*Lights fade.*)

END OF PLAY

www.ingramcontent.com/pod-product-compliance
Lightning Source LLC
Chambersburg PA
CBHW052220090426
42741CB00010B/2611